Heartfelt Leaders

AYMEN SAIHATI, MS

ISBN: 979-8-3864-9402-5

DEDICATION

To all the leaders who lead and encourage with their hearts

CONTENTS

INTRODUCTION: THE HEARTFELT LEADER

"To command is to serve, nothing more and nothing less."
— Andre Malraux

"The secret of a leader lies in the tests he has faced over the whole course of his life and the habit of action he develops in meeting those tests."
— Gail Sheehy

"Yesterday I was clever, so I wanted to change the world. Today I am wise, so I am changing myself."
— Rumi

As a leader, it is essential to understand the importance of the role you play in the lives of those you lead. You must be able to inspire, motivate and lead with your heart.

The Heartfelt Leader is one who is passionate about the success of their team and leads through meaningful connections with people. The Heartfelt Leader understands that leading with compassion and understanding can create a productive and successful work environment. They strive to create a culture of trust and support, while understanding the individual needs of each team member.

The Heartfelt Leader is well aware of the power of their words and actions. They understand how to effectively communicate and listen to their team, while also setting a positive example for others to follow.

The Heartfelt Leader is not afraid to take risks and innovate. They are open to new ideas and creative solutions, and are not afraid to challenge the status quo. They are continuously seeking to learn and grow, and to push themselves and their team to the next level.

The Heartfelt Leader understands the importance of creating meaningful relationships. They recognize the value of investing in the people around them, and use this knowledge to foster a culture of respect and collaboration.

The Heartfelt Leader is an inspiring and motivating leader. They have an unwavering commitment to their team and their goals, and are passionate about leading their team to success. They understand that true leadership comes from the heart, and strive to lead with compassion and   understanding.

1 THE JOURNEY OF A HEARTFELT LEADER

"The secret of leadership is simple: Do what you believe in. Paint a picture of the future. Go there. People will follow."

— Seth Godin

"Tomorrow's leaders will not lead dictating from the front, nor pushing from the back. They will lead from the centre - from the heart"

— Rasheed Ogunlaru

The journey of a leader is never easy. It is a continuous process of self-reflection, learning, and growth. As a leader, you must be willing to take risks, make mistakes, and learn from them. You must also be able to inspire your team and push them to be their best.

Leadership is not just about giving orders and expecting your team to follow them. It is also about leading by example, setting a positive example for others to follow.

A heartfelt leader is one who leads with compassion

and understanding. They provide a supportive environment where their team can reach their full potential. At the heart of a heartfelt leader is the understanding that everyone has something to contribute.

A heartfelt leader takes the time to listen to the thoughts and ideas of their team and make sure they are heard. This leader is open to feedback and encourages team members to share their thoughts in order to improve the team's performance.

The journey of a heartfelt leader is one of continuous growth and learning. A heartfelt leader is never satisfied with their current level of performance and always strives to do better. They are open to trying new things and are willing to accept failure as an opportunity to learn and grow.

A heartfelt leader also understands the importance of relationships. They take the time to get to know their team and build trust. They recognize the importance of creating a positive environment where everyone feels appreciated, respected, and supported.

The journey of a heartfelt leader is long and difficult, but the rewards are worth it. With the right attitude and dedication, you can become an effective, inspirational leader who can make a lasting impact on your team.

2 THE POWER OF HEARTFELT LEADERSHIP

"The only safe ship in a storm is leadership."
— Faye Wattleton

"You must be the change you wish to see in the world."
— Mahatma Gandhi

The power of leadership lies in its ability to evoke emotion and bring people together in pursuit of a common goal. Leadership is not just about commanding and controlling, but rather inspiring and motivating people to strive for excellence.

Leadership is an art, one that is best expressed through heartfelt gestures. A leader who expresses genuine care and concern for their followers, who looks out for their best interests and is willing to invest in them, will gain their trust and loyalty.

Leadership is about creating a positive environment for employees to thrive in. Leaders who genuinely care about their team and demonstrate that through their words and actions will create an atmosphere of enthusiasm, motivation, and collaboration.

Leaders must also be mindful of the impact their words and actions have on their followers. Leaders should be aware of their own strengths and weaknesses and strive to use their strengths to build upon their followers' strengths and to help address their weaknesses.

Leaders should also strive to create accessible and positive communication channels for their followers. This will ensure that everyone is on the same page and have a clear understanding of the goals and objectives. Leaders must also be willing to take risks and make tough decisions. Leaders must be willing to push the boundaries and challenge the status quo in order to create a better tomorrow.

Finally, leaders must be willing to listen to their followers and take their opinions into account when making decisions. This will create a sense of trust and respect between the leader and their followers, leading to a more productive and successful team.

In conclusion, the power of heartfelt leadership lies in its ability to evoke emotion and bring people together in pursuit of a common goal. By expressing genuine care and concern for their followers, creating an atmosphere of enthusiasm and motivation, and being willing to take risks and listen to feedback, leaders can create a team that is both successful and enjoyable to work with.

3 BEING A HEARTFELT LEADER

"Become the kind of leader that people would follow voluntarily; even if you had no title or position."

— Brian Tracy

As a leader, it is important to remember that you are at the helm of a team. It is essential to lead with your heart, not just your mind. You must be able to empathize and understand the wants and needs of your team, and you must be able to demonstrate that you care about them.

Leadership isn't just about giving orders and expecting them to be carried out. It is about creating an environment of trust and respect within the team. People who feel valued and appreciated are much more likely to be loyal and productive.

A leader who genuinely cares about the team will foster a strong sense of camaraderie and motivate the team to reach their goals.

Leadership is also about leading by example. If you want your team to be successful, you must demonstrate the behaviors and attitudes that you expect from them. Showing respect for others and having a positive attitude will set the tone for the entire team. Encourage and praise your team, and always strive to provide them with the tools they need to succeed.

Finally, a leader must be flexible and open to new ideas. Listening to the team and considering different perspectives can help create innovative solutions. A leader must also be willing to take risks and try new things. This will set an example for the team, and help them to be more creative and innovative.

A heartfelt leader is one who leads with empathy, respect, and flexibility. By fostering a strong team environment and leading by example, you can create an atmosphere of trust and loyalty. This will help your team to reach its goals and become successful.

The Responsibility of Heartfelt Leadership: Understand your Role as a Leader

"One's philosophy is not best expressed in words; it is expressed in the choices one makes... and the choices we make are ultimately our responsibility."

—Eleanor Roosevelt

As a leader, it is your responsibility to understand your role and the impact your decisions and actions have on others.

The key to becoming a successful leader is understanding the importance of your role and how it affects those around you.

Leadership is not just about having the power to make decisions, but also understanding how those decisions will affect those who are affected by them. It is also about understanding the responsibility that comes with being a leader. You have the power to influence the lives of those who follow you, and it is important that you use this power wisely. You must take the time to evaluate the situation and consider the consequences of your actions. Ask yourself if the decision you are making is in the best interest of those you are leading. If it is not, then you should reconsider your decision.

Leadership is also about understanding the importance of communication. You must be able to effectively communicate with those who are following you in order to ensure that they understand your decisions and the impact they will have. It is also important to listen to the ideas of those you are leading in order to make informed decisions.

Finally, you should always strive to be a role model for those who are looking up to you. It is important to remember that you are a leader and should strive to lead by example. Set a good standard for those who are following you and never forget that you are responsible for the choices you make.

Leadership is a great responsibility, but it can also be an incredibly rewarding experience. If you take the time to understand your role, the impact it has on those around you, and the importance of communication, you can be a successful and effective leader.

Lastly, it's important to remember that not only leaders must know their responsibilities, but also followers have to know and understand the roles and responsibilities of their leaders.

4 LEADING WITH HEARTFELT PASSION

"The only lasting beauty is the beauty of the heart."
— Rumi

Leading with passion is the key to successful leadership. It is a skill that can be developed and honed, and it is one of the most powerful tools a leader can have in their toolkit. Leadership is about inspiring others to follow you and to believe in your vision. To be a successful leader, you must have passion for what you do and for the people you lead.

Passionate leaders have a clear and inspiring vision, an understanding of their own strengths and weaknesses, and the ability to motivate and guide the people they lead.

Leaders with passion are able to create an environment that encourages and supports the development of their team. They inspire their team by setting a good example and showing that they are passionate about their work. They are able to create an atmosphere of support and respect, and they are willing to take risks and make decisions based on their beliefs and values.

Leaders with passion also understand the importance of communication and collaboration. They encourage open dialogue and seek out the input of their team. They can also delegate tasks and provide feedback in a manner that is both constructive and motivating.

Leaders with passion foster a culture of trust and respect. They understand that their team is made up of individuals with different ideas, experiences, and perspectives. They listen to their team and create an environment of acceptance and collaboration.

Leaders with passion have a genuine desire to make a difference in the lives of those they lead. They take the time to understand and appreciate each team member, and they strive to create an environment where everyone can reach their full potential. Leaders with passion are passionate about learning. They are open to new ideas and are willing to take on challenging tasks. They are always looking for ways to improve their leadership and the team's performance.

Leaders with passion are willing to take risks and make difficult decisions when necessary. They understand that failure is part of the learning process and that success often comes from taking risks. They also understand that mistakes are part of the journey and that learning from mistakes is an important part of growth.

Leaders with passion are able to inspire and motivate their team to achieve great things. They create an atmosphere of trust and respect, and they foster an environment of collaboration and communication. They understand that success is a journey and not a destination, and they are willing to take risks and make difficult decisions when necessary.

The Art of Listening & The Power of Empathy

Humans have an incredible capacity for empathy and

understanding. We are able to see things from the perspective of another person, even if we don't always agree with them. This capacity for empathy is the foundation of effective leadership.

As leaders, we must be willing to listen to others and to be open to their opinions, even if they differ from our own.

The best leaders are those who are able to build relationships with their team members and to understand their needs. They have the ability to empathize with their team members and to make decisions that are in their best interests. This ability to empathize is also important in communicating with customers.

Leaders must be able to put themselves in the shoes of their customers and to understand their needs and wants.

Leadership is an art form, and the best leaders are those who practice it with an open heart and mind. They are willing to listen to others and to be flexible in their approach. They are able to make decisions that are in the best interests of their team and their customers. They are able to be human and to understand the needs and wants of those around them.

The power of empathy can be seen in how it helps to build strong relationships between leaders and their teams. Leaders who are able to empathize with their team members are better able to understand their needs and to create an environment of trust and respect. This trust and respect helps to foster a sense of community and collaboration between team members.

Leadership is not just about making decisions, but also about creating an environment of trust and understanding. Leaders must be willing to listen to their team members and to be open to different perspectives. They must be willing to empathize with their team members and to understand their needs. By creating this environment of trust and understanding, leaders can create a team that is inspired and motivated to do great things.

Communicating with Clarity & Positivity: The Power of Positive Feedback

Communicating with clarity and positivity is a key element of effective leadership. When we communicate positively and constructively, we create a more positive environment for our team.

Positive feedback is an essential part of an effective leadership strategy. It is important to recognize when team members are doing well, and to provide positive reinforcement.

Positive feedback is a powerful tool for motivating people and inspiring them to do their best.

The power of positive feedback lies in its ability to increase engagement, boost morale, and encourage team members to take ownership of their work. It is also a great way to show appreciation for hard work and dedication.

For positive feedback to be effective, it must be specific and timely. Make sure to provide specific examples of what team members are doing right, and make sure that they know how much you appreciate their efforts. It is also important to provide feedback that is balanced. Not all feedback needs to be positive – constructive criticism can help team members to grow and improve.

However, it is important to make sure that when offering criticism, the goal is to help the team member to become a better leader.

Finally, make sure to give positive feedback in public. This is a great way to show team members that you value their hard work and to motivate them to keep improving.

Positive feedback is an essential part of effective leadership. When used correctly, it can help to engage and motivate team members, boost morale and encourage ownership of work. When giving feedback, make sure to be specific and timely, offer both positive and constructive criticism, and provide positive feedback in public.

5 LEADING WITH A HEARTFELT VISION AND VALUES

"Good business leaders create a vision, articulate the vision, passionately own the vision, and relentlessly drive it to completion."

— Jack Welch

Leading with a strong sense of purpose and a clear vision of the future is a cornerstone of effective leadership. It is important to connect your purpose, vision, and values to the hearts of your followers.

A heartfelt leader knows that leading with passion, empathy, and enthusiasm can inspire others to take action and create meaningful results.

Leading with a heartfelt vision means having a clear picture of where your team should go, and how it should get there. It also means having a keen understanding of what matters most to your team and the people they serve. It's not enough to simply know where you're going; it's crucial to understand why it matters and why it should be achieved.

Leading with heartfelt values is equally important.

Values are the moral, ethical, and spiritual principles that guide our behavior.

A heartfelt leader will strive to ensure that their values are shared by their team, and that their team is living those values in their day-to-day actions. This requires a leader to have a deep understanding of their team's values and the impact those values have on their work.

Leading with a heartfelt vision and values can have a profound effect on a team's performance, morale, and engagement. When a team is driven by a clear purpose and unified by shared values, they are better able to work together to reach their goals.

By leading with a heartfelt vision and values, a leader can create an environment where everyone feels inspired to do their best work.

6 HEARTFELT LEADERS LEAD WITH RESILIENCE

"When we learn how to become resilient, we learn how to embrace the beautifully broad spectrum of the human experience."

— Jaeda Dewalt

Leadership is a challenging and rewarding journey. It requires a strong sense of resilience and a willingness to navigate the complexities of the journey.

Resilience is the ability to withstand and recover quickly from difficulties or setbacks. Leaders must be equipped with the right tools and strategies to build resilience and overcome any obstacle. This starts with having a clear purpose, understanding the challenges that come with the role, and being committed to learning and growing from the experiences.

Leaders must also strive to be mindful and present in their decision-making. It is easy to become overwhelmed by the situation and forget about the importance of staying focused on the goal.

Being mindful enables leaders to stay on track and

remain resilient in the face of adversity.

Leadership also requires strong communication skills. Leaders must be able to effectively communicate with their team and stakeholders to ensure that everyone is on the same page. This includes being able to listen to feedback and address any concerns in a respectful and productive manner.

Finally, leaders must also be able to foster an environment of trust and mutual respect. This means creating a safe space where everyone can feel comfortable enough to express their opinions and ideas. When everyone is able to contribute, it helps build a stronger team and a more resilient leader.

Leadership is a journey, and it requires resilience and determination. Leaders must be mindful, communicate effectively, and foster trust in order to build a resilient team. By doing so, they can lead their teams to success.

7 DEVELOPING HEARTFELT LEADERSHIP CAPABILITIES AND YOUR LEADERSHIP VOICE

"The growth and development of people is the highest calling of leadership."

— Harvey Firestone

Heartfelt leadership is about connecting with those around you on a personal level, and developing strong relationships that allow for more effective communication and collaboration. It is about understanding the needs of those you lead, and providing the support and guidance necessary to achieve the desired goals.

At the core of heartfelt leadership is developing the capabilities to effectively communicate, motivate and empower those around you. To do this, you must have a clear understanding of your own leadership voice.

Your leadership voice can be thought of as the unique perspective and approach that you bring to the table. It is the combination of your values, beliefs, and experiences that shape your outlook and define your leadership style.

In order to develop your leadership voice, you must

have a clear understanding of yourself and your capabilities. You must understand what motivates you, what drives you, and what you hope to accomplish. You must also have an understanding of the environment in which you lead, and the people you lead. This includes understanding their strengths and weaknesses, as well as their hopes and dreams.

The development of your leadership capabilities and voice should be an ongoing process. As you gain more experience and knowledge, you will begin to refine and hone your leadership skills. It is important to take the time to reflect on what has worked and what has not worked in your leadership journey. This reflection will help you to find ways to improve, and to better understand how to best serve those you lead.

As you continue to develop your leadership voice and capabilities, you must also remain mindful of the importance of empathy and emotional intelligence. Having the ability to understand and relate to the feelings and needs of those you lead will help to foster a sense of trust and respect. This will enable you to better serve those you lead, and to create a culture where everyone can thrive.

Finally, your leadership voice and capabilities should be used to inspire and motivate those around you. You can do this by sharing your vision and values, and by having an open and honest dialogue with those you lead. This will help to create an inclusive and supportive environment where everyone can work together to reach their goals.

By developing your heartfelt leadership capabilities and voice, you can become an effective and inspiring leader. You can create a culture of collaboration and respect, and make a lasting impact on those you lead.

8 EMPOWERING HEARTFELT LEADERS

"Great leaders can never go to the grave without empowering others. They empower others to lead before their time on earth is over because they understand that leadership is a baton that needs to be handed over."

— Gift Gugu Mona

"A true leader leads by empowering not by enslaving."

— Debasish Mridha

Leadership is all about empowering others. It's about giving people the opportunity to take ownership of their work and their lives. A leader must be present, engaged, and passionate about their role in order to truly empower those they lead.

A heartfelt leader understands the importance of empowering their team. They understand that their team members are the lifeblood of their organization, and they strive to create an environment that allows each individual to reach their fullest potential. They understand the power of collaboration, and they embrace the diversity of thought and experience that comes with it.

A heartfelt leader has a clear vision of what they want to achieve and works with their team to make it happen. They communicate their goals and expectations with clarity, and they are willing to listen to their team's ideas and feedback. When their team has a good idea, they are willing to take a chance and bring it to life.

A heartfelt leader is a mentor and a coach. They have the ability to motivate and inspire their team, and they are willing to give their team members the opportunity to fail and learn from their mistakes. They recognize the importance of providing feedback and constructive criticism and use it to help their team grow.

A heartfelt leader is a role model. They lead by example, demonstrating the same level of respect, integrity, and enthusiasm that they expect from their team. They are passionate about their work and strive to stay positive, even in the most difficult of times.

A heartfelt leader is humble. They understand that they cannot do it all alone and are willing to ask for help when needed. They recognize their own strengths and weaknesses and are willing to learn from others.

A heartfelt leader is confident. They know that they can achieve their goals and they are not afraid to take risks. They understand that failure is part of growth, and they use it as an opportunity to learn and grow.

In summary, a heartfelt leader is someone who is passionate about empowering their team, has a clear vision of what they want to achieve, and is a mentor and a coach. They lead by example, are humble, and are confident in their abilities. They understand the importance of communication and feedback, and are willing to take risks in order to reach their goals.

9 INFLUENCING HEARTFELT LEADERS

"In the face of leadership flaws, too many people assume cynical perspectives, rather than do the hard work of building relationships in which they can has a more positive influence."

— Ira Chaleff

Leadership is a powerful tool that can have a profound impact on those around you. As a leader, your influence can be seen in your team, organization, and even in the wider community.

Influencing others is an essential skill for leaders to possess. The most successful leaders are those who are able to influence others with their own heartfelt leadership. By instilling their own values and beliefs into their team, they can create an environment of trust, respect, and collaboration.

Leaders who are able to communicate their vision and inspire others to work towards a common goal are those that are most successful.

Leaders who are able to influence others with their own

heartfelt leadership understand the power of positive relationships. They foster open communication and create a culture of respect and mutual trust. They understand that effective leadership is about more than just giving orders, it's about creating an environment of collaboration and mutual respect.

When it comes to influencing others with heartfelt leadership, it's important to remember that it's not all about you. Leaders need to be able to listen to their team and understand their needs, wants, and desires. They need to be able to provide guidance and support while also encouraging team members to take ownership of their own actions and choices.

Leaders need to be able to recognize and reward the efforts of their team. They need to be able to provide feedback in a constructive manner and be open to constructive criticism. By praising team members for their accomplishments, leaders can create a positive culture that encourages creativity and innovation.

Leaders who are able to influence others with their own heartfelt leadership understand the importance of leading by example. They strive to be the best they can be and they lead by example, inspiring others to do the same. They also understand that mistakes and failures are a part of the learning process and they use them as opportunities to grow and develop.

Leaders who are able to influence others with their own heartfelt leadership understand the importance of self-care. They take time to rest, reflect, and recharge in order to stay focused and motivated. They understand that the most successful leaders are those who are able to lead with their hearts and minds, and who are able to inspire others to do the same.

Leadership is a powerful tool that can have a profound impact on those around you. By influencing others with your own heartfelt leadership, you can create an environment of trust, respect, and collaboration. You can foster open communication, create a culture of respect and mutual trust, and help your team to take ownership of their own actions and choices. You can help your team to recognize and reward their efforts, provide feedback in a constructive manner, and be open to constructive criticism. You can lead by example, inspire others to do the same, and take time for self-care.

By utilizing your own heartfelt leadership, you can be a positive influence on those around you and help your team to reach their goals.

10 CREATING A HEARTFELT CULTURE

"Part of company culture is path-dependent -- it's the lessons you learn along the way."

— Jeff Bezos

The workplace is the foundation of any successful organization, and creating a culture of respect and empowerment is a key factor in fostering collaboration.

Respect and empowerment are not just words, they are attitudes and behaviors that create an environment that encourages collaboration.

When creating a culture of respect, it is important to recognize and appreciate the value of each individual's contributions.

Respect is not just about being polite, it is also about recognizing the unique talents and abilities of the individuals within the organization, and giving them the opportunity to share their ideas and work together to achieve a common goal.

Empowerment is closely related to respect, as it is about giving individuals the freedom to express their ideas, take initiative, and take ownership of their work.

Empowerment also encourages collaboration by giving

individuals the opportunity to work together to solve problems and develop innovative solutions.

Creating a culture of respect and empowerment requires a commitment from every individual in the organization.

Respectful communication is essential in fostering collaboration, and leaders must be role models for this.

Leaders should demonstrate respect for each individual and their contributions, and encourage an open dialogue that encourages everyone to participate.

Leaders must also provide clear direction and guidance and ensure that everyone is treated fairly and equitably. This includes creating a safe environment where individuals feel comfortable expressing their ideas and opinions and know that they will be accepted and respected.

Ultimately, creating a culture of respect and empowerment is an ongoing process. It is an investment, and it will take time to build a culture where everyone feels respected and empowered. But by recognizing the value of each individual's contributions and creating an environment of respect and empowerment, leaders can foster collaboration and create a workplace that is conducive to success.

Always remember, your organizational culture and environment are the mirror of the organization's leadership attitudes and practices.

11 THE HEARTFELT LEADER'S IMPACT AND LEGACY

"My jobs as a leader is to make sure everybody in the company has great opportunities, and that they feel they're having a meaningful impact."

— Larry Page

As a leader, your impact and legacy are critical to your success. It is important to remember that what you do and do not do today will shape the way you are remembered tomorrow.

Leadership is about making a difference in the lives of those you lead and serve. You can do this by setting an example of how to lead with a compassionate and heartfelt approach. You don't have to be perfect; you just need to be authentic and honest in the way you lead.

The heartfelt leader's impact and legacy will be determined by their ability to make a positive difference in the lives of those they lead. It is not enough to simply be a good leader; you must strive to be an exceptional leader by inspiring and motivating those you serve.

When leading with a heartfelt approach, you will be mindful of the impact your actions have on others. You will take into consideration the long-term effects of your decisions, and strive to make decisions that will benefit your team and the organization as a whole.

Your legacy as a leader will be determined by the way you have used your power and influence to make a positive impact in the lives of those you lead and serve. You will be remembered for the way you led with integrity and passion, and for the difference you made in the lives of those you led.

Leadership is not a one-time event; it is a lifelong journey. The heartfelt leader's impact and legacy will be determined by their commitment to making a difference in the lives of those they serve.

Your legacy and the impact of your leadership will be felt long after your time as a leader has passed. As leaders, we all strive to make an impact and create a legacy.

The heartfelt leader is no different. In order to create a lasting and meaningful impact, the heartfelt leader must first understand the power of their own emotions.

Heartfelt leaders know that their emotions drive their decisions, and they use this knowledge to create positive outcomes. They understand that their feelings and reactions can shape the environment they are in and the people they interact with.

When making decisions, heartfelt leaders take the time to consider the impact that their decisions will have on those around them. They consider the long-term implications and the potential for growth and development for those in their care.

When it comes to creating a legacy, heartfelt leaders understand that it is more than just words. They strive to make a lasting impression on everyone they interact with. They use their experiences and emotions to create an environment of trust, respect and understanding.

To ensure that their legacy lives on, heartfelt leaders

strive to develop relationships that will outlast their own.

They use their emotional intelligence to build strong relationships with those in their care and to nurture those relationships long into the future.

Heartfelt leaders also recognize that their legacy is about more than just their own influence. They understand that their legacy will be determined by the actions and accomplishments of those in their care. Therefore, they strive to ensure that their mentees and other followers have the resources and understanding needed to create their own legacy.

The heartfelt leader's impact and legacy is an important part of their overall success. They understand that their emotions can have a powerful influence on those around them, and they use this knowledge to create a lasting and meaningful impact.

By considering the long-term implications of their decisions and nurturing relationships with those in their care, heartfelt leaders can ensure that their legacy lives on long after their own life has ended.

12 OVERCOMING CHALLENGES WITH HEARTFELT LEADERSHIP

"When it's tough, will you give up, or will you be relentless?"

— Jeff Bezos

As a leader, it is not uncommon to face challenges in our work. Whether these come in the form of difficult conversations, difficult decisions, or difficult circumstances, encountering these moments can be difficult.

However, with the right tools and mindset, we can learn to overcome these challenges with heartfelt leadership.

The foundation of heartfelt leadership is understanding and valuing each person we interact with, no matter their position. This means that each person we encounter is worthy of respect and kindness.

We must strive to treat each person as an equal and valuable part of our organization. This helps to create an atmosphere of respect and trust, which can be invaluable when it comes to overcoming challenges in the workplace.

The next step in overcoming challenges with heartfelt leadership is developing a mindset of resilience. Resilience is not just about enduring difficult times, but also about learning from them. By reflecting on our experiences and understanding what we can improve, we can become stronger, better leaders.

We must also remember to recognize when we have done well, to help us stay motivated and confident.

Finally, it is important to be proactive when it comes to addressing challenges.

This includes keeping open lines of communication with our team, staying organized, and being prepared for any situation. By being proactive, we can be more confident in our decisions, and better equipped to handle any situation that arises.

Heartfelt leadership is about more than just overcoming challenges; it is about creating a culture of respect and trust. It is about understanding that each person we interact with is valuable and worthy of respect. It is about finding strength in adversity and being proactive in addressing any issues that arise. With these tools and mindset, we can become more effective and successful leaders.

13 MAKING DECISIONS WITH HEARTFELT LEADERSHIP

"You have to enable and empower people to make decisions independent of you. As I've learned, each person on a team is an extension of you're leadership; if they feel empowered by you they will magnify you're power to lead. Trust is a great force multiplier."

-- Tom Ridge

Leadership is a complex role that requires making decisions that are not always easy. It is important for a leader to be able to make decisions with their heart as well as their head.

Leaders must be able to consider all aspects of a situation and make decisions that are in the best interest of their team and organization.

At the heart of heartfelt leadership is the desire to make the best decisions for the team and organization. Heartfelt leadership requires leaders to take a step back, look at the situation from all angles, and assess what will be best for the team.

Leaders must be able to put aside personal biases and be open to input from all members of the team. Leaders must also be able to make decisions quickly and confidently.

Making decisions with heartfelt leadership requires taking into account all the facts, considering different perspectives, and then making a decision with conviction. A leader must be willing to stand behind their decisions, even when they may not be popular. Leaders must also be willing to accept responsibility for their decisions.

Heartfelt leadership requires leaders to recognize when a decision was wrong and take ownership of the situation. Leaders must be willing to take corrective action if necessary and be open to feedback from the team.

Finally, leaders must be able to evaluate the impact of their decisions. Heartfelt leadership requires leaders to assess the outcomes of their decisions and learn from their mistakes.

Leaders must be able to reflect on their decisions and make adjustments as needed. Making decisions with heartfelt leadership is a complex and challenging task. It requires the leader to be aware of their own feelings and biases, be open to input from others, and be willing to accept responsibility for their decisions. By using these strategies, leaders can become more effective and make decisions that are in the best interest of the team and organization.

14 LEADERSHIP LESSONS OF HEARTFELT LEADERS

"Teh greatest leader is not necessarily teh one who does teh greatest things. He is teh one that gets teh people to do teh greatest things."

— Ronald Reagan.

Leadership is an ever-evolving art form. It requires an understanding of the people you lead, and a willingness to learn from the experiences of others.

Heartfelt Leaders are those who take the time to understand their constituents, and who lead with a passion that comes from within. These leaders recognize the importance of developing strong relationships with their followers, and work to cultivate an environment of trust and respect. They understand that their actions will have a lasting impact on their followers and strive to make the right decisions.

Heartfelt Leaders view their followers as individual people, rather than just numbers. They take the time to get to know their followers, and learn what motivates them. They use this knowledge to create a positive and meaningful working environment, and to ensure each person is given an opportunity to grow and develop.

Heartfelt Leaders also understand the value of collaboration. They recognize that working together can create a synergy that leads to greater success. They work to foster a culture of collaboration, allowing their followers to work together to develop solutions and reach their goals.

Finally, Heartfelt Leaders understand the importance of taking risks. They recognize that taking risks can lead to greater rewards, and are willing to take calculated risks to reach their objectives. They also understand that mistakes can be learning opportunities, and use them as a way to grow and improve.

Heartfelt Leaders have a deep understanding of the people they lead, and use this knowledge to create a positive and meaningful working environment. They also recognize the importance of collaboration and taking risks, and use these tools to help their followers reach their fullest potential.

CONCLUSION: FINDING YOUR TRUE NORTH

"You're task is not to seek for love, but merely to seek and find all the barriers within yourself that you has built against it."

— Rumi

As a leader, it is essential that you consistently strive to find your True North. This is the point in your life where you have the greatest clarity about what you want to achieve, the values you hold and the impact you want to have.

When you are aligned with your True North, you will have the confidence and conviction to make decisions that are in line with your values and that will lead to the greatest good for all involved.

The journey to find your True North is not always easy. It requires you to take time to reflect on your life, your experiences and your values. It means being honest with yourself and embracing change when needed. It also means staying true to who you are and standing firm in the face of adversity.

Finding your True North can be a lifelong journey, one that requires dedication and commitment. But when you stay focused on your values and purpose, you will find that your path will become clearer and your decisions will become easier.

As a leader, staying connected to your True North can help you to stay true to your purpose and make decisions that are in the best interest of all.

At the end of the day, it is up to you to find your True North.

This journey is yours and only yours to take. As you travel along your path, remember that it is never too late to start and that it is never too hard to make the necessary changes to stay true to your values and purpose.

Finding your True North is a process, and it is one that can bring you great clarity and joy.

HOW CAN I HELP?

As a leadership expert, it is my passion and ambition to encourage individuals to achieve their goals, whether on a personal or professional level.

At MARKO Advance, we provide Consultancy, Management Development, and Disruptive Business Solutions. We also have many international and regional partnerships that enable us to have a huge team of local and international experts. Our skilled staff can advance an organization's work and enhance its performance by offering creative, practical, and long-lasting solutions, as well as scientific research, practical strategies, and clever programs.

Reach MARKO Advance via:
Email: hello@markoadvance.com
Website: http://markoadvance.com/

BOOK AYMEN SAIHATI TO SPEAK AT YOUR UPCOMING EVENT

You won't find someone more considerate, respectful, and enthusiastic about leadership than Aymen when looking for a professional speaker for your upcoming event. Aymen will present a tailored message that will be helpful in working with well-known CEOs and having a beneficial influence on colleagues and communities' leadership and work environment, whether your audience is in the Middle East or abroad. Aymen shares his knowledge in an effort to strengthen the person's leadership qualities.

Aymen Saihati is a resourceful, innovative, goal-oriented, energetic, and dynamic leader and recognized globally and one of the global Gurus in Startups specializing in Training and leadership development by the Global Gurus Organization.

Aymen provides services and expertise to several organizations and individuals and when you hire Aymen, he will present a deliberate and all-encompassing leadership strategy that will have a significant effect on the audience. He is aware that your audience either already leaders or aspiring leaders, will discuss to them about how to innovate as a leader and how to offer management solutions to organizations.

"My Mission is to help my Clients to Build & Create their Impacts and Legacy"

— Aymen Saihati

You may reach me at:
Email: aymen@aymensaihati.com /
aymen.alsaihati@markoadvance.com
Address: P.O Box 784 Postal Code 31972 Saudi Arabia
Websites: http://markoadvance.com/,
http://aymensaihati.com/
LinkedIn: @aymensaihati

THE AUTHOR STORY

Aymen Saihati, the Founder, CEO and Chief Visionary Officer of MARKO Advance. Incepted in 2019, MARKO Advance is a leading Consultation and Management Development firm that provides Consultancy, Leadership & Management Development, Cultural Transformation, Disruptive Business Solutions, and represents international experts based in Dammam, in the Kingdom of Saudi Arabia.

The Beginning of the Entrepreneurial Journey

Aymen is a professional expert and facilitator from highly-recognized and top-ranked organizations, including Leadership Management International (LMI)-USA, PECB-Canada, and MARKO Advance-KSA. He had helmed and aced multiple roles and responsibilities during his long and illustrious career. His educational background includes a Master of Science Degree in Psychology, a Bachelor's degree in Clinical Laboratory Sciences, and an Organizational Leadership Certificate. Aymen also working on his DBA degree.

However, the idea of becoming an entrepreneur and having his own business had always chased him when he was a regular employee who was neither satisfied with his job salary nor with the development, he was having compared to what he had always imagined. "I have always wanted to do more in my life, and explore those areas in my life that I have always been curious about. I wanted to have a better understanding of my abilities and skills, and unleash the knowledge, experience, and personal leadership style that I have always seen different from anyone else," shares Aymen.

What supported his idea and encouraged him, even

more, was the severe need he noticed in the market which made him more passionate to seize the opportunity and help. This led to the birth of MARKO Advance (MA), a business that started from zero and has lived for 3 years in the business and still living and surviving, yet more passionate and ambitious.

Creating a Difference through Advanced Services

Attaining a distinctive niche in the competitive market can be a daunting task for most ventures. However, MARKO Advance has successfully overcome this hurdle through its distinct and advanced services. Built on the core values of teamwork, innovation, and rigorous dedication, this customer-centric firm is specialized in 5 key areas: Leadership Development, International Keynote Speakers and Experts, Cultural Transformation, Coaching, and Retreats. MARKO Advance provides effective leadership development programs that lead to the desired and predetermined goals. Aymen is one of the main leadership experts in the MARKO Advance Team and also the author of several books that will be published within 2023. Currently, he is working on a book that talks about why leadership development programs and initiatives fail. MARKO Advance is also connected to international experts from around the world with possible opportunities in Saudi Arabia & GCC. It is helping organizations with the cultural assessment, mapping, and transformation. Additionally, MARKO Advance provides several types of coaching sessions for groups and individuals and it delivers and coordinates retreat sessions and activities inside KSA and abroad for companies and organizations.

Besides these key areas, the organization also focuses on B2B & Business to Non-Profits services and outsourcing and supplying for other training and consultancy practices. "MARKO Advance could be the perfect place for advanced services that keep us unique and different in our field and totally scientific and evidence-based. Another thing is having highly effective facilitators, consultants, and specialists in unique areas, as well as, introducing new services and international experts to Saudi and GCC markets," elucidates Aymen. MARKO Advance always keeps its team, leadership methodology, consultancy, management development, and services up-to-date and cooperative with the best global experts. It makes sure whatever it provides is flexible to the market's needs, besides being on the same level of proficiency it is reflecting. Moreover, the company provides Management Development, Consulting, Tailored Solutions, Professional Certifications, Digital Reality, Assessment Tools, and other services on request.

The Magical Ingredient in MARKO Advance's Success Formula

An amiable and collaborative work culture is one of the key elements for establishing professional production and growth. As a firm believer in this philosophy, MARKO Advance strives to cultivate a people-centric work culture by taking care of its team. At MARKO Advance, each employee is appreciated for the invaluable expertise and knowledge he/she brings to the table. The firm keeps its team's mentality positive and clear by providing them with a convenient and positive working environment to produce the expected excellent work. "We believe that taking care of our team is one of the key elements for establishing professional production and growth because they are the magical ingredient in our success formula," asserts Aymen.

The company supports remote working to provide convenience to each team member to match their lifestyle while offering them different development opportunities and tracking their growth in terms of knowledge and skills. As for the emotional side, MARKO Advance pays great attention to their team's emotional state, as it plays a vital role in their growth as well as the development of the organization by motivating and supporting them towards doing their best. Embracing their thoughts and opinions strives to make them feel involved and encouraged while understanding their personal life and circumstances to build a relationship of trust, flexibility, and professionalism with them.

Building a Defined Culture and System of Leadership

As the CEO and CVO of MARKO Advance, Aymen is responsible for leading the business and people, setting the direction, determination, and continuity, developing relationships, closing sales, providing the necessary support to his team and business, and converting it into a sustainable business. "My mission is to help clients make impacts and legacy," states Aymen. He further adds, "One of my primary responsibilities as an entrepreneur is to learn from the market, our performance, experiences, and mistakes. We need to cultivate what we are learning to make better decisions for our business continuity and sustainability."

According to the ardent leader, good leadership is about leading people and building a leadership system within MARKO Advance that effectively applies to a defined culture and system of leadership. "However, a good leader should begin with me from the inside. So, personal leadership, including mindset, attitudes, and character, is essential for any leader. As a leader, I have to lead my team to achieve predetermined goals, visions, and strategies. As a small business entrepreneur, only I have had to simplify all procedures and tasks to be easy to understand and apply," he adds. For his valuable contributions, Aymen has been included in the most lucrative yet pervasive list of Top 30 ranking of Global Gurus and attained the rank 19 in the start-up category 2023.

Set to Expand the Horizons

Under the indomitable leadership of Aymen, MARKO Advance is growing at a rapid pace and plans to reinforce its growth in the forthcoming years. Now, it is completely focused on and working its way to provide its services to more clients in Saudi Arabia and all GCC countries as well as doubling the efforts to expand and reach more prospective clients in some developing countries in Asia and Africa. "It is essential to mention that we see these goals we decided to choose to share as some of the great steps towards reaching what we are aiming for, which is becoming the source of change, development, and innovation that will no longer reach but to be reached," he affirms. The company is happy to deliver its services to all companies interested in having its services. Also, it is able to bring the best international experts to all interested organizations. Its unwavering commitment to the clients and hassle-free services leads the company towards mammoth success.

AYMEN SAIHATI, MS